THE
TESTING GROUND

P. S. Miller

WESTBOW
PRESS

A DIVISION OF THOMAS NELSON

WestBow Press books may be ordered through booksellers or by contacting:

WestBow Press
A Division of Thomas Nelson
1663 Liberty Drive
Bloomington, IN 47403
www.westbowpress.com
1-(866) 928-1240

Because of the dynamic nature of the Internet, any web addresses or links contained in this book may have changed since publication and may no longer be valid. The views expressed in this work are solely those of the author and do not necessarily reflect the views of the publisher, and the publisher hereby disclaims any responsibility for them.

Any people depicted in stock imagery provided by Thinkstock are models, and such images are being used for illustrative purposes only.

Certain stock imagery © Thinkstock.

ISBN: 978-1-4497-1389-8 (sc)
ISBN: 978-1-4497-1390-4 (e)

Library of Congress Control Number: 2011923715

Printed in the United States of America

WestBow Press rev. date: 3/22/2011

CONTENTS

PREFACE

This is a first book for me. I had contemplated writing this book for over ten years. I am a medium, I communicate with the spiritual realm and the spirit realm communicates with me. My gifts are God given, extraordinary, paranormal. I am able to hear the dead, the angels and also the negative forces or spirits of the universe. I have seen the face of God. I have seen the "Evil One." What I am revealing in this book will be difficult to believe.

As a medium, I have the ability of clairaudience. I hear with a "psychic ear". I can hear voices that vibrate at a higher frequency. I also have the ability of clairsentience, which means I can sense when a spirit or spirits are in a room. I can see spirits or scenes that flash in my mind. This is known as "clairvoyance". I am aware that I am not alone. There are many other mediums throughout the world. There is a television program based on a real life medium, called "Medium". I have read all of James Van Praagh's books and admire his abilities and how he has helped countless bereaved persons heal their grief with his readings. However, in the Bible, Leviticus (20:6), New Century Version, the Lord Almighty says, "I will be against anyone who goes to mediums and fortune tellers for advise, because that person is being unfaithful to me." I don't think the Lord meant he would damn anyone for eternity, but he wants you to come to him with your troubles, believe in, trust in him foremost, show him love, reverence and obey his laws.

My hope is that my book will give you, the reader, more peace, hope and joy, knowing that God and Jesus do exist and that this life we lead on earth is but a temporary one, the "testing ground" for the more permanent spiritual one we will live in heaven. Thus, the title of my book, "The Testing Ground", is based on my own personal experiences as a medium. When I conveyed my thoughts, concerns, fears about writing this book to my guardian angel, his question was, "Are you ready to die?" My reply was telepathically, "Of course not!" I have much I want to do! I have family, work, so much I wish to do and see!" His response: "Tell them what you know!" And that is exactly what you will read in the following pages. I think the angel asked me that question because many are suffering, facing certain death and still wonder if there is something beyond this world. I believe they want me to relate my personal experiences to give comfort to those persons.

CHAPTER ONE:
FIRST ENCOUNTER

My first encounter with seeing spirit was when I was about 12 years old. My father died a slow painful death of cancer. He was dead about three days, when late at night, as I was trying to fall asleep, I looked up to see my father before me, not far from the foot of my bed. He was standing there surrounded in a bright light. He appeared much younger, wearing a white button down shirt and light colored pleated slacks. I was so astounded I did not know what to think. He smiled at me, appeared happy and seemed to be conveying that he was fine and that life goes on in spirit. What is particularly eerie, is that years later I would find one of the only photos of my dad with his father and brothers and the way he presented in the photo was about the same in his presentation to me after his death in spirit! I must admit that I felt comforted but at the same time, somewhat fearful. I believe he came back to comfort me because a year or so prior to his death I confided to him my fear of dying and that death might mean the very end, in the grave. I remember really pondering about death. When I was about 11 years old, I passed by a large cemetery with my Girl Scout troop. I recall that I began to feel quite melancholy, wondering about my existence and would I cease to exist after my physical death? I communicated this to my father and he just joked about death and tried to get me to lighten up. Several weeks after his death, I went to Virginia Beach to visit my brother and his family with my oldest sister and her fiancé. I remember as I lay on the couch, the nearby rocker was moving, creaking and going back and forth. I was starting to feel somewhat afraid, but remembering my previous encounter, felt strongly it was dad, letting me know he was with me, to watch over me. For years after his death I could sense his presence in the house. I could hear his footsteps, his cough. I knew he was nearby, to watch over me. Many years later an angel would just say his first and last name to me, further verifying yes, he is in heaven!

You see, what I have come to realize is that we are "energy". We need our physical bodies while we are earth bound to tool about the earth, but when the body dies as it surely will, "our energy", which is our soul is free to ascend to heaven.

Another experience in my late teens had reinforced this. I was close to awakening and felt my spirit lift out of my body and hover near my body! I recall my brain thinking that my body was just an empty shell or warehouse for my soul. I remember I just thought of my body quite impersonally, as if it were just a thing I needed while I physically existed. This experience happened in seconds and no, I did not have to die to experience this! I heard a famous medium who almost died and left her body, recount that she looked down on her body and appeared to feel much the same way I did, quite impersonal, describing it, the body, as a "thing". This was indeed an important learning experience in my spiritual growth, a lesson my angels wanted me to learn.

CHAPTER TWO:
ANGELS/ANGEL ENCOUNTERS

I have a guardian angel; he gives his name as Gabriel. I see my angel most every morning and evening when I retire. I have very strong visions with my eyes closed. Some visions are so vivid, most are in color and are like looking at a television screen with your eyes open. Some of the images are hazy and some very clear. My angel has wings and is surrounded in a very bright white light. I feel him as a male presence, his voice sounds male and he appears to look male with dark hair. I have had female sounding voices come through as well and seen angels that were definitely female.

About seven or eight years ago, while my eyes were closed, I experienced a vision. It was very vivid and quite astounding. It was a band of angels flying together! They all appeared to be male, they were all wearing long flowing gowns, a beige or off-white color, and yes, they all had wings! I could not believe this experience, it was so incredible. Yes, dear reader, angels do exist!

Angels are messengers from God. Many philosophers and religious leaders of ancient times told of angelic encounters. Plato, the Greek philosopher, said that by meditating on the light in one's head, a person could make contact with celestial beings. Angels are sent to earth to guide and protect us. Angels can guide you by implanting ideas in your mind. Such as when you have a strong inclination to take a different route from home only to find out later, had you not, you might have been involved in a terrible accident. Hearing voices often means the presence of angels, especially if the voices carry a ringing or bell like quality to them. I experienced this bell like ringing on many occasions when heaven was communicating with me. That definitely got my attention! One of the most profound was when I had finished viewing the movie, "The Passion of Christ". After watching the film, I went upstairs to my bedroom, turned on the light and sat on the bed, when suddenly I heard this strong ringing in my ears for a few seconds, then a voice came through very loud and clear and said, "Hi Pam!". It appeared to be a female voice and the angel was seemingly conveying that heaven was very pleased and overjoyed that I watched this film. I almost did not watch it because I of course heard about the violent beating of Jesus. Well, I must say to Mel Gibson that as most of the public applauded the film, heaven did as well!

Another encounter occurred some years ago when my husband and children were out of town. It was the middle of the night and I thought I heard the front door rattling! I then heard these voices saying my name over and over, "Pam, Pam!" But I had taken an Excedrin PM and was resisting coming awake. The next morning I noticed a light snow had fallen and there were large cowboy footprints in front of my front door and in front of my garage! Someone, it appeared was outside in the night trying to get in and when I did not awake, I have no doubt my angel scared him off!

I am sure that angels exist. Many times as I was driving home from work as a crisis counselor at 2:00am or later, I would almost doze off and felt someone, press against my shoulder, and awaken me to full alertness! I feel very strongly, that many nights, especially when driving on ice and snow packed roads exhausted, that without the protection of my guardian angel I would not be here today or may have gotten into a serious accident. Another time was when my daughter was ill one night. I was sleeping and sometimes I put my arms above my head and I suddenly felt two distinct taps to my arm, right near the elbow. It semi-awoke me and I remember thinking, "who was that?" and then awoke to find no one in the room. I started to fall back asleep again and about fifteen minutes later my daughter came in my room and told me she was very sick and vomiting. I asked her if she had just come in the room earlier and she stated she had not. My husband was not in the room, he was out of town. I administered some medicine to her and she was able to return to bed.

Another time, I remember thinking that I hope I can get up earlier this morning and color my hair and make it to work on time. I set the alarm and fell back asleep and I had my knees up while sleeping and felt the flat of someone's very large hand firmly tap on my knees two times. I thought to my self, why is he waking me up and then I heard him say, "It is 4:45am". I then turned and looked at the clock and sure enough he was right. It was 4:45am, the time I wanted to get up! It was my guardian angel helping me to get up on time, conveying he knew my wishes and that he was there to help and support me!

I am sure you heard about the "Missouri Miracle". Two boys that were missing were found! When I heard about Ben Ownby abducted after being dropped off his school bus I was horrified and extremely concerned, as were many. I prayed fervently that God would guide law enforcement to find him as soon as possible. I know more than most, the horrors that the young man could be facing and its lasting devastating psychological effects. I remember I was out walking on my break from work around noon and I said to God, please God send an angel to guide law enforcement to notice the identified vehicle the perpetrator was driving and then locate the evil person who abducted Ben. I stated this to God in a very demanding voice, "I want Ben out of there today!" I stated this many times, not aware that Sean Hornbeck would be found as well, the very day I asked, no demanded the rescue! I am not taking credit for the Miracle alone, it was my prayer and the many thousands praying that brought this to pass! When I heard the news on the radio on my way home that very day, I was totally euphoric! I ran in the house and shouted, "Praise the Lord!" That night I received a beautiful vision, three angels, were smiling and dancing about! They were the most beautiful I have seen thus far, with long beautiful shining hair and the most gorgeous faces. I remember thinking they were far prettier than any super model I have ever seen! I recall I was thinking I wish I could look half as pretty! This was a message from heaven! They were happy for the boys and their family reunited and letting me know that God was listening! Sean and Ben know that God loves you and the evil Michael Devlin will face the wrath of God like no other!

More recently, some months back, I had gone to the movies at the mall cinema with my daughters and grandson. It was a very cold blustery day and I was racing back to my van to unlock the doors and get the heat going. As I frantically attempted to get the key in the lock I banged my hand hard against the door on the driver's side and before I opened the door, I noticed that the center stone was missing! I remember distinctly that the stone was in the ring while in the movie theatre. The stone is very prominent and I was wearing my glasses, as I always do, and they magnify everything many times their original size. I recall sitting there as I often do, admiring the way the dimmed lights cause the rings to sparkle ever so beautifully while I wait for the movie to start. My ring is designed to look like a flower, with a larger center stone and three smaller petal-like stones on each side. I was almost in a panic, searching for the stone, looking on the ground, and then when I looked inside under the steer column, I saw two bright sparkling stones! I examined both stones and was puzzling as to why I found two stones, as only one was missing and they looked identical! I quickly put the two stones in a small plastic bag. I could not understand how the stone that was present in the ring while I was in the theater could possibly be now found on the floor of my van. Weeks went by and my daughter and I went to Cape Girardeau, two hours from my home, where my jeweler, Rogers Jewelry is located. I called them ahead of time and arranged to have them repair the ring. When I arrived the lady there examined both stones and one was determined of course to be real and upon closer examination under the microscopic lens the other not a real diamond. When driving home that day I was indeed feeling very blessed and grateful to my angel and to the wonderful jewelry repairman who did such a wonderful job restoring my ring to it's almost new-like splendor! My daughter and I were chatting, driving along and suddenly my daughter said "mom, look at that rainbow!" It was off to my left and it was like no other I had ever seen, it was shaped like a ring! And reader, let me stress it had not rained in days and it was over 85 degrees! Later, as I was reading the Bible I was astounded to read this passage in Genesis (9:12-15), New Century Version "And God said, 'This is the sign of the agreement between me and you and every living creature that is with you. I am putting my rainbow in the cloud, as the sign of the agreement between me and the earth. When I bring clouds over the earth and a rainbow appears in them, I will remember my agreement between me and you and every living thing."

Dear reader, Guardian angels often, as I have indicated, helped others. In the magazine; "Woman's World" there is an article 'My Guardian Angel". In this article readers share their experiences about how their guardian angel has helped them and many of them related how their angel helped them find a missing ring or diamond. I read in the June 15, 2009 article how a woman from Hillsborough, NJ, had for years not been able to afford an engagement ring and finally her husband took his bonus money and bought her the ring she longed for. The article related while on a cruise some time later she looked down and notices the diamond was gone! She reported she and her husband re-traced their steps and back to their room and then later that evening when near the pool she looked down and there was her diamond! How she wondered? The deck was washed down, hundreds of people passing through! Dr. Doreen Virtue, PhD, author of 30 books on mind-body-spirit topics, including "My Guardian Angel: True Stories of Angelic Encounters from Woman's World Readers and host of the Internet radio show "Angel Therapy" says that "Diamonds are a symbol of the strength of a marriage" and whenever someone would ask Heaven to help them find a missing stone, the angels will find a way to bring it back to them. Oh yes, reader, as I have stated earlier, I realize I am not the only medium and I realize that I am not the only one who has had an angel encounter!

CHAPTER THREE:
PRESENTATION OF GOD AND JESUS

As I have communicated, I talk to heaven, and heaven talks to me. Heaven has strongly conveyed to me that Jesus is the Son of God. I have seen God and Jesus together, Jesus to his right. I have seen the face of God Almighty! I have seen God presented to me alone and I have seen Jesus alone. If I were an artist, I could paint them! The Lord presented to me in a vision. Remember dear reader, that when I have these visions, I am usually not asleep, though some do present prominently in dreams. I am generally awake and they present while my eyes are closed and I am in a completely relaxed state and are like looking at a television screen, most times the images are very clear and detailed. I see them with my mind's eye. This vision of God was in color, the most beautiful colors, the best I can describe is to say pastel colors. He is surrounded by a brilliant light. His hair was long, straight to his shoulders, salt and pepper, mostly gray. He had no beard or mustache. His face was somewhat round and he smiled at me with the sweetest and warmest of smiles. He did not say anything then, he did not need to. The look he gave me made me feel so loved. Prior to this encounter an Angel conveyed to me saying; 'God loves you, Pam!" This I have known all my life, but hearing it from heaven, seeing his face was so awesome! Why me? I would wonder. Yes, just another being on the planet. I've always strived to be a good person, was confirmed in my church in my youth. I often helped the elderly in my neighborhood. I was in nursing school for a brief time and helped nurse the ill, some of them terminal. Later I would become a professional counselor and guide many to get help before they would kill themselves by their own hand or with drugs and alcohol. I have done much good in my life, but I am far from perfect. I have a temper and curse at times. I am sometimes impatient with others and do not even go to church every Sunday. I go to church generally only on Easter and Christmas day! But, I appear to have found favor with God! I feel very blessed and I know with every fiber of my being that God exists, and that Jesus is his son. Jesus, the greatest teacher that ever lived! He sent us the most important message anyone could ever utter from his lips, "For God so loved the world that he gave his one and only son, in order that anyone who believes in him won't perish but will have eternal life!" Of course in our world many turn from goodness and the light of God to one of darkness and evil. They will not see heaven; they will not obtain life eternal. When Jesus presented, he was dressed entirely in white, with a beautiful glowing light about him. His hair was a rich deep dark brown, almost black and he had a very full beard and mustache. He did not say anything at that time. Prior to his presentation to me an angel a few weeks before, just stated the name, "Jesus". What struck me most was the way the light played off his hair. I remember thinking he is a very pleasant looking man, his hair is so beautiful and shiny, and like none I have ever seen on earth. He smiled sweetly. I heard a voice say, "Jesus, teacher" and a few weeks later God would speak to me for the first and only time thus far and stated to me, "He is my son!" So, dear reader, this was all so very awesome, to hear from God himself, what I already strongly believed with all my heart and soul. So those who do not believe, take heed, this is the truth, it comes from God himself. He tells no lies, he loves you! But should you not fear him and not accept Jesus as his son, you may miss out on eternal life in heaven.

Another day Jesus presented to me and I have made note of the date because it was such a profound experience, not that the others were not equally profound, but I just made an effort to write it down it was June 13, 2008. I was lying on our loveseat in my living room and was seated somewhat upright watching television. It was about 9:30 pm and I began to doze off and had fallen asleep but soon began to awaken and was about to open my eyes when I saw Jesus. He was seated, he appeared to be dressed all in white, the long robe over top a long gown and he looked very tall, about 6'4" or more would be my guess. There were others in the background but I could not make out who they were and frankly Jesus was my main focus as I was so astounded to see him again so prominently. The vision faded and likely lasted about 10-12 seconds and I was so tired I walked straight to my bed and as I was about to lay my head on the pillow, Jesus said he would help me and proceeded to state my first and last name. He had heard my most recent fervent prayer as I was struggling with some upsetting family issues and many times almost in tears asked Jesus to help me and this was just a few days before he appeared to me! My husband was about to have major surgery and I had really little support except from my grown children. Jesus knew this and wanted me to know he cared and all would be well. My husband had his hip replaced, recovered beautifully and has stated he did not have any pain whatsoever! Praise God, praise Jesus, his only Son, our Savior divine!

I remember when I went for a walk, not long after we moved to Belleville, IL and I was feeling very sad and alone and in tears asked Jesus and God to be my friends, as I was feeling there were very few people I could count on lately. This is when one morning when I awoke, I had first seen God and Jesus together. Later, after moving back to St. Louis, before I fell asleep one evening, I heard Jesus say, "Good friend", then later on a few mornings he would say, "Good morning!" and I would automatically say, "Good morning" back and realize after I said that, that I was just talking to the Son of God! One time recently when I started buying lottery tickets, Jesus said with a laugh in his voice, "So who wants to be a millionaire?" He definitely has a sense of humor! God and Jesus both have many of the emotions and feelings we have: love, happiness sadness, anger, jealousy. Remember, Jesus was human and the Son of God. He lived among us for a time. Dear reader, both are capable of great empathy and tenderness but can become very angry and enraged by man's continual wickedness and downright stupidity!

CHAPTER FOUR:
ALMA CURED

I lived in Indiana and I was 29 years old and working as a psychologist at Evansville State Hospital, when my sister Alma, two years older, called and told me she was just diagnosed with ovarian cancer. She told me a large cancerous tumor was found on her ovary. This would not have been detected, had she not had extensive tests to determine why she was not able to conceive. When I got off the phone with her I went straight to my bedroom, got down on my knees and prayed to God to save my sister and give me a sign that she would be all right. While I prayed I felt a strong presence. I felt God in heaven, actually was listening to my prayer and I felt very comforted. My sister would go through an operation to remove the tumor and I drove up to her home in Kentucky to visit with her when she got released from the hospital. While I was there, her in-laws were also visiting. I did not know them well, so looking back on this, I can not believe why I would suggest to her mother-in-law that we should play the word game, "Boggle". If you are not familiar with this game, it is a game where you shake up this small box of cubed letters, sit it down ,put the glass timer over and try to make up as many words as you can by looking at the case of letters and how the letters connect before the sand runs out. I remember I shook them up quite well, sat down the case, opened the lid, and saw the words: "tumor dies". I recall looking at her mother-in-law in astonishment and awe and she looked back at me surprised and we never spoke of it since. I, being the spiritual person I was and am, with my previous encounters, knew this to be the sign I was waiting for from heaven. My sister went on to have many radiation treatments and she has been cancer free ever since. That was well over twenty years ago! Praise God from whom all blessings, miracles flow! I think God was particularly touched by my genuine love and heartfelt desire to save my sister as she, while we were growing up, often was mean to me, bullying me when I would not do what she wanted me to. But I still love her, though to this day, we do not often speak to each other or spend much time together.

CHAPTER FIVE:
COMMUNICATIONS FROM MOTHER

My mother was the salt of the earth. She was a good mother and had a hard life. She only had an eighth grade education, was naïve in some ways, almost child-like at times, but generally very shrewd and very wise. I was very close to my mother. She was very different after her heart surgery, seemed at times more irritable and depressed. She lived in a senior high rise by herself. My older sister cared for her often when her health grew more fragile. Eventually mom would need to be placed into a nursing home. She became very thin and fragile toward the end. It was so sad seeing her decline. She was always so independent and resourceful. I remember the last time I saw her in the nursing home, she was sleeping most of the time but when I was about to leave she was sitting on the edge of the bed, looking so small and helpless. I had to return to St. Louis, to my work, my life and family there. It broke my heart to leave her! I had a feeling that I might never see her again. I gave her a warm hug and said my good-byes. It wasn't long afterwards that she died and unfortunately I could not be with her at the end but my elder sister was. The bonds of love never break and my mother would be in touch. She would communicate with me from the other side! My mother strongly believed in the afterlife and in God. She related to me communications, signs she received when some of her relatives had died when I was little. When I was living in my new home in Belleville, IL, a year after she died, I was resting, reading in my formal living room. It was daytime and I was to go to work that afternoon. I worked as an evening crisis counselor for a managed care company. I was very relaxed, not asleep, when I heard a voice, my mother's most distinctly say, "Hi Pam!" She sounded so happy, so joyous! I could easily detect this in just those two words. I sat up and smiled and thought, "Aha!" today is my mother's birthday! I had forgotten about it until she communicated with me! She wanted me to know she was happy and doing fine on the other side! Another time thereafter, I was in my dining room, petting my fluffy cat, Rusty, stating out loud, "Oh mom, you would love this cat. I wish you could see her!" Then suddenly, right after I made that statement, the dining room chandelier light came on all by itself! The light is turned on by a dial across the room. There was no one at home but me. As I indicated before we are "energy" living in physical bodies and after death we are energy and can travel as we wish and can communicate in many ways, many times through electricity. So many times I could feel my mother's presence. A few times the television in my bedroom would light up on its own, without being turned on. So comforting knowing she was happy on the other side! So good knowing she was watching over me, sending her love from beyond. I realize some of you love going to the gravesite and talk to your deceased loved ones. While a gravesite visit can be comforting, only their remains are present. They are in heaven and can be brought closer if needed. You can send your love in your prayers, at church or at home and they will listen, love hearing you talk to them and tell them about your hopes and dreams.

When my mother was alive she sometimes would ask me to buy some gifts for family members from her. The first Christmas after my mother died I decided to send some Christmas presents to my sister and her family and this time I put from grandma. I wanted to honor her with this. I did not care how strange it would appear or 'crazy' this may seem. As I was wrapping the gifts I heard an Angel say to me; "She likes this!" 'You are one of the best!" And later the angel said my father's first and last name. I was so touched, heaven approved, my mother approved and my deceased father. It touches them when we do things to remember them, honor them and are good to each other!

CHAPTER SIX:
STANLY, "I WANT TO BE HERE"

Over three years ago my brother-in-law, Stan was diagnosed with lung cancer. He was a heavy smoker for a majority of his life. After being diagnosed, he died four months later, as he had stage IV lung cancer. The night before I got the news he died, as I was awakening I heard a voice say, "Sorry, funeral." Often my messages from heaven are very short, comprised of just a few words or one sentence. I then saw a beautiful angel in a gorgeous filmy flowing dress, with long hair in a plait down her back. She was doing this incredible ballet-type dance. It was so relaxing and comforting watching her! I then got up when she faded away and went out to the kitchen. I heard the phone ring and answered it. It was my sister, Karen, tearfully relating to me that Stan had died yesterday. While he was ill we had kept in fairly close contact but the last I had heard he was not doing that badly, the swelling had gone down from his face and he was eating better. Of course, having had the warning of a death earlier in the morning from heaven, I was not totally surprised. It was November, cold and dreary, threats of rain, sleet and snow, but I assured my sister that I would book a flight and be with her as soon as possible. I flew out that evening. She resides in Ohio and I flew into Columbus airport and rented a car. It was dark and the anxiety was building so I played some tunes on the radio as the rain and sleet slashed at my windows. I felt very alone as I turned onto their small rural road and then looked up in amazement because as I turned into the road, on the right side, stood about twenty or more deer staring at me most serenely as if to say, "Welcome, we were expecting you!"

I continued to drive cautiously along; their home was just a mile or so up the road that is fully wooded on both sides, for a few miles and a creek running to the left. When I approached her long graveled driveway I was even more astounded! It was almost surreal. On both sides of the driveway stood about twenty to twenty-five deer. They looked at me so sweetly and serenely and seemed to be my "welcoming committee!" When I emerged from my car I was noisily dragging luggage etc from the back of the car and trunk. I was slamming doors and all the while, the deer stood steadfast, just watching me intently, not moving a muscle! I had a sense that God himself had sent the deer to welcome me. He knew I was feeling scared and all alone, so just as he sent the dancing angel earlier, he sent the deer to me!

It was so sad the first day Stan was laid out at the funeral parlor. His sister Pat had leukemia and it was her birthday! Karen and I bought her some gifts to let her know we cared and told her to open them some day when she was up to it. Then there was Mary Linda, Stan's sister-in-law, battling cancer for the last few years, a tube in her chest to administer her medication! I walked over to her, she was sitting and I bent down, clasped her hand and told her how sorry I was of Stan's passing and her own stress, dealing with her illness and softly, calmly related that I was praying for her.

This was all too much for one family! Stan dies, his sister and sister-in-law both battling cancer! It was a very depressing situation all around and their home, in that dark depressing area, so many old dark buildings and her home down that lonely country road. It was so different from St. Louis, Missouri! That night at her home it was difficult to fall asleep but I had a vision of Stan on the other side. He was looking very young, early twenties, dressed with his hair combed back and wearing those pegged leg pants, waiting by a door. He appeared to be waiting for someone to come for him and I did not hear a voice but a strong psychic message came through from him, "I want to be here!" I related this to my sister and it seemed to give her some comfort. Mary Linda would die a year later in the summer in July. I was in Las Vegas, Nevada with my husband. That is right, 'sin city'! As I was awakening that July 4th morning I heard the strong bell-like ringing I had heard before and I knew it was heaven calling. No, reader, it was not from a late night of heavy drinking! I had a glass of wine with dinner and retired about 11:30pm. I am not a wild party person. After the ringing I heard a voice say, "Hi Pam!" It was a female voice and it sounded very familiar. I began to think of whom it belonged to and I thought of Mary Linda! I did not know she was dead or near death, as far as I knew she was responding well to her treatments. When I got home, and a few weeks had gone by, my sister told me that Mary Linda had died and she said she was buried on July 4th! I instantly realized that the voice I had heard was hers! She was 'happy' on the other side! July 4th had been one of her favorite holidays. She always threw the most incredible parties, so I bet she had an even more incredible one in heaven!

Let me stress this clearly, heaven is an awesome place, no I have never been there but once I saw Jesus kneeling looking out over a high bluff. I saw clouds in the sky so I have to assume heaven resembles earth, but is far more beautiful than we can imagine and those that pass over are delighted, no 'ECSTATIC' to be there!

CHAPTER SEVEN: FAMOUS ENCOUNTERS

I remember sitting at work and had read on the internet news that John Ritter had died. I suddenly remarked after reading this to my co-worker, "Oh no! John Ritter died, I love that guy!" It was a straight from the heart feeling. I really did admire him. He was a very talented and versatile entertainer and appeared to have a good heart, a decent human being and wonderful family man too. The next morning as I was awakening, I heard a man say, "Thank You!" That is all he said but it sounded distinctly like John Ritter's voice, as I've heard it hundreds of times watching his shows. He had that little laugh in his voice and he sounded as did all the others who came through, "ecstatic" to be in heaven! Its beauty is unfathomable and you know you have eternal life in paradise, what is there not to like?

I have also heard an angel say "Gregory Peck" not too long after his passing. Heaven knows I greatly admired him as an actor and human being. He appeared to be loaded with charm, elegance, and to be a true gentleman. Moreover, I saw Michael Landon on the other side. He was smiling broadly, had on a white shirt, looked very young, very happy. He appeared to be standing on a small bridge.

I have also seen John Kennedy Jr. He appeared to be wearing a maroon shirt and tie and appeared to be giving a talk. This was not long after 911. Another time I saw a vision of his plane shooting like a missile, straight into the ocean and he then stated sadly, his wife died. He indicated he observed his cremation and started to joke about it but I conveyed I did not want to know more. I think he brought this up because he knew I harbored fears about that, though I knew from my psychic abilities and experiences it was nothing to be fearful of. I guess I am because that would be the very end of my physical existence on the earth and there is the realization there is no turning back to all that you have ever known. Another time he conveyed to me he missed Caroline and thought of her often. He conveyed 'classroom' with the message, so I assume he meant his fondest memories of he and his sister was when they were learning together in a classroom.

One time I heard Jackie Kennedy's name mentioned and I did see a very slim attractive woman with big glasses. She was far away. The image did not come in very clearly but it did appear to be her. When I queried was that "Jackie?" a few nights later I saw a paper in a vision, her name written over and over, many times! I guess they were saying "Yes you silly!"

More recently when I was arising for work, I had heard a man say, "You are a romantic!" "Watch the 'Long Hot Summer!" I adore classic old movies and began to brainstorm, repeating the title over and then I realized that sounded like Paul Newman and that is a Paul Newman movie! Paul had just died about three weeks ago. It was Paul communicating from Heaven! Paul adored his beautiful, talented and devoted wife Joanne, and I feel he was sending this message for her as this I believe was the first movie they made together and fell more deeply in love. I have always been a big fan of his and am happy to know he is sending his love to his dear wife and is happy in Heaven. Paul Newman was not only a huge talent, but a spectacular human being. He gave back to those in need and is surely special to God!

When Heath Ledger died it really disturbed me, as it did of course his dear Michelle and sweet daughter, family and millions of adoring fans. I thought he was very talented, handsome and a unique individual, though, clearly going through a very tough time psychologically and emotionally. I remember seeing how happy he was when he was with his little 'Matilda'. After he died I asked God to send his best guardian angels to watch over his little girl and Michelle. Not long after I made this request I saw Heath in a dream, In the dream, I was parking my car in the lot at work and Heath was in a car facing me with that big smile on his face, looking so happy! And I think I know why, he was touched by my care and concern about how he died so tragically and my concern for the dear ones he so loved and had to leave behind.

Later after Charlton Heston died, before falling asleep one night I saw a clean shaven man who looked like Charlton. I did not see his whole face, but most of it and it did appear to be him. He looked to be early 30's, very handsome indeed. Remember dear reader, in Heaven, you are renewed and most choose to be young again, looking better than ever!

CHAPTER EIGHT:
DEMONIC ATTACK!

You have probably heard about the movie, 'The Exorcist' or have seen it. I certainly will never forget the experience! It was one of the scariest movies I have ever seen. I was eighteen and attending nursing school and was dropped off at home by my boyfriend after the movie. I was all alone in the house and it was difficult to fall asleep that night as I could remember the creepy voice that was Satan's and it was terrifying. Many years later I would be working at the 'new' Alexian Brother's Hospital, built on the very grounds where the old hospital was, the one where the actual exorcism took place. Of course in the movie it was a teenage girl but in real life it was a fourteen year old boy. The boy went through much terror and torment before the Devil was released from him. Fortunately, the exorcism was a success. The boy awoke after ten weeks period of exorcism, stating he had a beautiful dream in which a man in white with a "glowing" sword of flames drove the demons down into the pit. The Brother had asked if the man identified himself and the boy said he called himself, "Michael". The boy was free of the symptoms there after. Make no mistake, dear reader, evil does exist, the Devil does exist, he is not a cartoon character or a myth.

The Devil does exist and his demons are at play throughout the world, perhaps more noticeably in Iraq. The Garden of Eden was in Iraq and Satan made his first appearance in Iraq. As I have indicated earlier, we are not our bodies. We are energy and the Evil One is attracted to negative energy, the hatred that man espouses for his fellow man is ever so strong in that part of the world. Suicide bombers blowing up the 'innocents' and they have the nerve to refer to their war as Jihad or a "Holy War!" It is anything but, it is not and their reference as such is a blasphemy, heaven tells me. God is not behind their wicked cause, the devil himself is! The Devil wants them to destroy each other! He is constantly stirring the pot! I say let's all make Satan cry! Let us put down our weapons and talk of peace!

I have told you that I have seen God, Jesus, some of heaven and the angels. I have also seen the Devil! I had a strong vision of him, he was galloping in the netherworld. I saw him from behind. He was half beast, half man and appeared reddish in color. So much for the phrase, "devil red". There appeared to be clouds of mist rising about him in the vision. I have also seen his demons, a band of them, marching together, all in black, and each carrying an inverted cross! It was not a pretty sight to be sure.

So there we have it, Good and Evil, God versus Satan! Make no mistake, God is on our side and it is high time we were more on his! One great vision I had was of a beautiful tree and in the tree was a huge feather. The feather was a brilliant red, white and blue! The psychic message Heaven was conveying appeared to be that God upholds, supports, and loves America! So, I ask you dear reader, Why can't we say the pledge of allegiance as I did in my school days; "One nation under God!" People, let us get this straight, that is why God helped us be the mightiest nation on earth, because he knew we would be a people that would help those weakened by evil regimes and oppressed, without the fruits that democracy can give.

More personally, I have been under demonic attack. It is not a pleasant experience, trust me. A few years back, while at my sister's visiting, I awoke in the morning and while walking to the bathroom I heard the distant strong bell-like ringing and then a man's voice very distinctly said to me, "He will try and hurt you!" I believe this was Jesus. I was not sure exactly what he meant by this but a few months later I was to find out. The attack was most intense for almost three days. I was experiencing vile persistent thoughts about my children of which I now do not remember or care to. Being a mental health clinician, it was like suddenly having an obsessive compulsive disorder, but I knew better, I was not mentally ill, I was under attack! While this was happening I kept thinking to myself it was 'Hell' literally! I went to my car on my break and the car was parked, motionless and all of a sudden a bird flew directly into my windshield and splattered dead on the car! I prayed to God to help me. I read the Bible, particularly the Psalms and it stopped.

But there were other encounters. One early morning when I was awakening, I heard a man call me some vile names. One night later my teenage daughter and I were alone at home, downstairs in the family room watching television. It was about 9:00pm and suddenly we heard someone rattling the front door handle, like they were trying to get into the house! My husband and son were out of town and we were not expecting my older daughter who lives on her own. We immediately sprang from the couch, bounded up the stairs. My daughter grabbed a ball bat and I, my cell phone, opened and ready to dial 911. I yelled out, "identify yourself or get off my property! I'm calling the police!" Before I yelled this, the rattling was going on as we initially approached the door. I had a distinct feeling; there was no human person on the other side of the door! I called my neighbor and she said her husband was out walking the dog. That dog is so hyper, if any person were at my door, the dog would have barked his head off! Early the next morning when I was awakening, I heard a sinister voice state very clearly, "I hate women!" I have no doubt who said this, it was Satan! Well, let us look at some parts of the world where women are treated like they are indeed hated! Let us look at Iraq, Iran, Afghanistan, Africa, and North Korea, just to name a few! These are clearly the Devil's playgrounds! Another time he stated he, meaning, Satan, could read my mind and I thought, "so what!" I thought, not much exciting there, work what chores need doing, what to have for dinner! But reader, please take note; you never want to be engaging in communication with the Devil! That is most dangerous territory! Another time because his occasional taunts, foul names, etc were not working with me, he stated, "I will find some way to get to you!" Keep in mind dear reader, the Devil can not make you do anything you are not willing to do. I believe I read that Andrea Yates, who drowned her five children, indicated she was tormented by the Devil, and he allegedly told her, he could read her mind! I have no doubt what so ever that what she experienced was torment from the Devil. Remember he and his demons are attracted to negative energy and thoughts but did the Devil make her drown her children? I think not! I speculate that she was indeed severely depressed and angry toward her husband who kept making her pregnant though doctors strongly advised against her becoming pregnant after the third child, that she just went over the brink! But, alas ultimately the blame goes to poor Andrea, she knew right from wrong, but was too depressed, angry and unable to control her actions at the time. She likely saw those children, at that time, as obstacles, not human beings.

So, the closer we are to God, the farther we are from evil, the Devil and his influences. When we love God, acknowledge Jesus, as his son, follow his commandments, we generally have good thoughts about ourselves and life in general and do not engulf ourselves in hatred and evil.

CHAPTER NINE:
PETS LIVE ON!

My cats are precious to me. I treat them as though they were my children. I often pick them up, kiss them, and tell them how wonderful they are and how much I love them. I have lost pets and it was very painful. I had a cat, Rudy, and he died after fourteen years. When Rudy passed over I could hear him purring and felt his presence in the house after his death. I could see his 'cat spirit form' on the ceiling in my bedroom most mornings! It was a somewhat dark mass of energy shaped like a cat! Sometimes when I focused on him, I would observe him doing the usual cat things, such as cleaning his face, chasing his tail! It was very comforting and astounding that I discovered that I had this ability, given to me by God. Later I would get another cat, Rex. Rex was a Maine Coon cat, very handsome, smart, and affectionate but at times could have anger outbursts. He was very jealous of the new cat, Rusty. Rusty was a beautiful female, long haired cat I got later. Rex lived about eight years and when he was six years old he was diagnosed with diabetes. One day he was sleeping on the back deck and it was daytime and we had to run to the store for an hour. We thought it would be all right to leave him sleeping peacefully on the deck. When we returned we could not find him and we were frantically searching and calling for him to no avail. Later, from a neighbor's report, it appears Rex may have been kill by a coyote. About six months later, it was early morning and I was alone in my bedroom, the door shut and I could feel a cat drop from the ceiling and land somewhat heavily on my bed! I then distinctly felt the cat walking about the bed, kneading the comforter with its paws and purring! I opened my eyes and looked about, but saw nothing. I would have hundreds of these encounters with Rex. As I indicated earlier, I am able to see the 'cat spirits' on the ceiling. I realize this sounds very 'far out', but I am able to sense the deceased cat's presence.

Later on, my beloved cat, Rusty died shortly before Christmas 2006. She had developed kidney failure. We are not sure how, as she was always so healthy, but it was around the time they were recalling some tainted cat food. I cried so hard as she was such a lovely golden beauty. I used to refer to her as my "teddy cat" as she was so soft and cuddly like a little teddy bear! A week after she was gone, I asked God to show me Rusty on the other side. Oh and before Rusty died, about a month before a strong message came through, "Sorry Andrea". I began to fret, surely heaven is not conveying that something bad will happen to my dear Andrea! Later when Rusty died, I realized they were warning me Andrea would have the hardest time coping with the cat's death and this was certainly the case. But God did answer my prayer! I asked God to allow me to see Rusty on the other side and I did! A few days later I received a beautiful vision from heaven. I saw my beautiful golden cat, fluffy tail fanned out, straight up and she was surrounded by a beautiful glowing light. She looked very healthy and very alive! I then saw Rusty run to a rather tall angel and jump into his arms! I then observed the angel lovingly petting my deceased cat, alive in heaven! The cat appeared most happy and content. I immediately felt very comforted. Of course given my experiences so far, as a medium, I knew she lived on, but this is just what I needed. There are days when I really miss Rusty, but when I do, I call upon the vision, still very vivid   in my mind and I find instant comfort.

In the Sunday St. Louis Post Dispatch, February 8, 2009, I read a letter to Dr. Fox, a veterinarian. In the article/letter, the writer states he was meaning to write ever since he read in one of his columns about woman who saw her dog after his death. The writer stated he has a similar experience when his beloved cocker spaniel, 'Casey' at age 13, who had many medical problems and he put her to sleep which was not an easy thing to do as the dog had seen the writer through a divorce and several moves. The writer stated that one particular night while crying very hard, the writer screamed, "Casey I want you back!" Then a few nights later she came to him. The writer indicated that he was "sitting on the bed, kissing and petting her" He related she did not speak to him but conveyed she was happy, safe and no longer in pain. The writer said, "It was so real, I could actually feel her." Dr. Fox thanked the writer for the letter and thanked the many readers who sent him often-vivid accounts of their deceased cats and dogs manifesting in various ways!

So, pet owners enjoy your pets while you can but don't despair as like your family and friends, who pass on, your pets will be waiting to welcome you on the other side when it is your time to move on!

CHAPTER TEN:
TERROR IN THE WORLD: GOOD VS EVIL

Dear reader, soon after we invaded Iraq, I received an astonishing vision. I had a strong vision, it was, as I had indicated, much like looking at a television screen. In this vision I saw Osama Bin Laden sitting with a much older man. They appeared to be outdoors and it was evening. They were seated low to the ground. They both wore those turban headdresses and were arguing vehemently with each other. Believe me, if any of what they were saying, or any tips of their location were revealed to me I would certainly have conveyed this to the proper authorities, but it was not. The message from heaven appeared to be that God has his eye on them and they will not escape his wrath! Also it was conveyed that they are running scared, very terrified because the United States invaded Iraq. The stupid fools thought all of their cowardly tactics, suicide bombings of innocent women and children, and the be-heading the innocents would cause us to back down; well they just don't know what we are made of! We are the greatest country on the planet, with the strongest, bravest soldiers in world! God made this country and the people in it strong and he will never allow any terror group, any hostile country or their fanatical hate mongering leaders to bring us down!

I had a strong vision. Oh reader, it was very powerful and it was "so real". I saw many women and children running and screaming in terror for their very lives! Then an angel said: "missiles, Iran!" That was all they conveyed and that spoke volumes. Heaven is warning us emphatically about what we already know and fear. Heaven is telling us that Iran is a threat to world safety and cannot under any circumstances be trusted at all. What we've been reading, hearing about, their building of nuclear weaponry and missiles is very scary and Heaven knows they cannot be dealt with diplomatically. Reader, let's get this straight, you can not have diplomacy with radical power hungry, hate driven irrational leaders like President Ahmadinejad of Iran. Yes, we as Americans are tired of hearing about the loss of lives in the war on terror. There are many brave soldiers that have been killed in Iraq, Afghanistan and other dangerous places in the world, where we are trying to promote democracy and decent treatment of fellow human beings. We must, however, remember that over 4,000 Americans died on our soil! They were just like you and I, went to work to try and support their families and they never got to come home! Kudos to the brave military, ours and the other great God fearing countries of the world that are not going to let these thugs go unscathed! Let's not forget that since 911, we have been safe and many Al Qaida thugs have been either incarcerated or eliminated thanks to the decisive leadership of President George Bush! Hail to the former Chief! No, we have not yet managed to catch one of the most evil beings on the planet, Osama Bin Laden, but remember dear reader, he may escape justice in this world but he will not in the next! As Jesus had said, "What profited a man to gain the world and lose his soul?" You have one God given soul, one chance on earth to prove you are worthy to come to Heaven and if killing, maiming and torturing innocents is more important than eternal bliss in Heaven with your family and loved ones, then by all means carry on and see the consequences! When Osama faces God, the Almighty, ruler of the universe, he will know a terror unlike no other he has ever known. God will likely make him see and feel all the pain his evil has caused before he destroys his very soul! He will not exist. He will be nothing! Reader that is what happens to those who continually chose evil over goodness and mercy. In the Bible, Matthew; "The way to Heaven is hard. The gate is wide and the road is wide that leads to Hell, and many people enter through that gate. But the gate is small and the road is narrow that leads to true life. Only a few people find that road."

CHAPTER ELEVEN:
BROTHER JAMES

My brother James was diagnosed with pancreatic cancer, July 2005 and in November of the same year, a few months later, he was dead. My brother was 61 years old when he died and was eleven years older that I. We were not that close. I was a child when he left and joined the Navy. He married not long after joining the Navy and had three sons and a daughter. I saw little of him over the years, as he lived in Virginia and I was in West Virginia. I met his wife and children and saw them on rare occasions. We talked on the phone a few times prior to his death. My two older sisters planned to visit him and did so prior to his passing. I did not see him before he died. I regret now, that I did not make the time. But, brother did not appear angry as a few days before Christmas he said, "Merry Christmas!" He was doing well on the other side! Before he died he was sounding so brave, he would forego the chemo and try to live out the days left without any extra stress and pain that would not likely save him anyway. He had stage IV cancer. After he died I received the longest message from Heaven; they said they were very pleased with how I handled myself in the past three days. It was very comforting, the kind words from Heaven and my brother's cherry greeting! So, dear reader, if you have a loved one, you've lost touch with, please don't let too much time go by. It might be too late and you could have had so many meaningful interchanges that would likely enrich your life, your very soul! Think about it! When you die, there is no coming back! You have one chance to get it right! There is no reincarnation. The only times people come back after death and become others or an animal is in the movies! It is a fantasy. God gives you one life to live, one soul to a person. You don't get any chances to come back and get it right. This is the "testing ground" for eternal life. So, as I indicated, I have my regrets and the best thing we can do for ourselves in this life is to learn from our mistakes. In Heaven there will be no material wealth, you leave the fancy mansion, cars, wardrobe behind. You bring your soul, the true essence of your being. What is important is how you love others and the sacrifices you make. So my message to you: love your family, cherish your time together, and love and fear the Almighty and accept Lord Jesus, his son and you will have eternity to continue to share love!

CHAPTER TWELVE:
MORAL DECAY, NOTHING SACRED

The television shows of today are so radically different from the wholesome television I viewed as a child. When I reflect on the entertainment that the media provides today, I think, shades of Sodom and Gomorrah. It appears that today virtually anything goes. The so called "reality" television programs are mostly, in my opinion, "trash TV" I have to wonder if most of the writers are still on strike! Or most so strung out on drugs that they lost all of their creativity? Thank goodness for TV Land, so I and other Americans, not totally morally bankrupt, can view some decent programming! I'm sure Satan would approve of the show with the bisexual woman who in one episode, encouraged the raunchy competitors for her 'affections' to act like writhing possessed freaks in a cage! Make no mistake, Satan is for evil and moral degradation in any form, God, on the other hand, is for good and moral behavior. So, dear reader, if you are for God, decency and promoting the uplifting of morals in our beloved country, take the time to write to advertisers, television stations, letting them know they have gone too far! Dear reader, those who would do anything to make money do little to enrich their lives or souls. We know that some put making money, gaining power and status over all else. While their bank account rises, their soul shrinks! But let us be sure about this, those that do, will have little to no status or standing in God's kingdom!

We all know the evils of child abuse, whether it be physical, verbal, emotional or sexual. I ask you dear reader, "What is the most precious thing you have besides your very life?" If you think along the lines of material wealth think again! It is your 'peace of mind!' I have counseled many a person, victims of various types of abuse and perhaps the worse is sexual. To take away a child's very sweet innocence is a crime that should be payable by death! Many, I have counseled told me I was the first person they could tell! They were feeling so dirty and ashamed they could not even tell their own parents. In many cases, it was their own parent or parents who abused them! Can we even imagine what that must be like for an innocent helpless child? The very person, who is supposed to protect and shelter them, is abusing their own flesh and blood! Satan is smiling, but God and Jesus are not amused! In Matthew (18: 5-7), New Century Version: "Whoever accepts a child in my name accepts me. If one of these children believes in me, and someone causes that child to sin, it would be better for that person to have a large stone tied around the neck and be drowned at sea. How terrible for the people of the world because of the things that cause them to sin. Such things will happen, but how terrible for the one who causes them to happen!" Take heed Al Qaida, taking young innocents, young children and training them, forcing them in your evil doings. Forcing them to kill, become suicide bombers! You shall forfeit your very soul and burn in the fires of hell! Is your evil hate mongering really worth your very soul?

So you, dear reader, can make a difference! Don't rent or buy movies degrading women and children. Stand up for those weaker than yourselves. As I indicated earlier, Satan said to me, "I hate women!" In Afghanistan and other depressed nations, women are treated like dirt, as are the children. Those who perpetuate this evil will find no favor with God!

The internet brings much knowledge to us with a click of a mouse, typing a few words on a computer screen, but as we are finding out the internet holds great evil, pornography, promoting moral corruption and spreading hate and evil. Those who use it for thus, will not escape God's wrath. He knows all! He sees all! In Matthew: verse 15: Jesus said, "Listen and hear what I am saying. It is not what people put in their mouth that makes them unclean. It is what comes out of their mouth that makes them unclean." "Out of the mind come evil thoughts, murder, and adultery, sexual sins, stealing, lying and speaking evil of others. These things make people unclean."

So the message to the hate mongers, those with racial prejudice. If you survive God's wrath and enter the kingdom of Heaven, which is highly unlikely, you will see all those you wronged, the Blacks, Hispanics, and Chinese and so forth, all people of various races will be in heaven. They will be there for all eternity! There will be no blowing them up! Burning them up! No way to destroy them! They will have the eternal sanctity of God's Kingdom if they have loved and feared the Lord and followed his commandments and accepted Jesus, as God's son. The Lord Almighty made many different races with many different cultures to make the world a rich, interesting and a diverse place. He has hopes that mankind will treasure and learn from our differences and enrich our lives, not plot and plan how to destroy each other because of the differences! That dear reader is Satan's hope and plan and many are eagerly following it, much to their own demise!

This is the testing ground! Those who follow the wide evil path will travel to Hell. Dear reader, Hell is not a pleasant place. Heaven loves my description or analogy of what if will be like for those who relish evil. Picture if you will that it is a stifling hot day, about ninety-five degrees plus and you are sitting in your car. You have options, roll down the windows, turn on the air conditioner, open the doors, to cool your overly hot body. On the other hand, imagine if you do not have these options! (Oh yes, particularly you witless persons who have left a helpless child or animal locked in a vehicle!) Yes, imagine that you indeed have no options! You cannot open the door! The windows will not open and you cannot turn on your air conditioner! You are stuck! No options, no way out! You are hot and oppressed with no one to turn to, no one who cares! And if that is not bad enough you have you have Satan laughing loudly, saying, "I've got you now!" I've got you now!" over and over, for all eternity!

So my advice for all of you who are sinning, doing evil, turn away, run to God, repent before it is too late and you face eternity, that is forever and forever without options, without God and Jesus.

CHAPTER THIRTEEN:
ABORTION IS KILLING

Abortion is a highly controversial subject and some at the far left think that a woman should be able to have an abortion, no matter what stage the pregnancy, for whatever reason she chooses and at anytime she deems it necessary. Then there are many religious conservatives who staunchly believe life begins at conception. They believe in the sanctity and protection of all living things and that abortion should be outlawed in and under all circumstances. For many abortion is the taking of a human life and most Christians believe life is sacred and a blessing. Abortion is synonymous with killing. The Commandment, "Thou shall not kill" is fervently obeyed by most of us, but does God mean we should never kill? Of course not! If an intruder bursts into your home and states he will kill you and rape and murder your children and you have a gun handy, God would not fault you for defending your home and those you love by killing that evil person. I don't have all the answers but I feel that like killing, God would forgive abortion if it is only carried out just like any "killing", only under extreme circumstances. We sanction killing in war, threats to our safety and life, these are extremes. In extreme circumstances, such as a rape, molestation or if a woman's life is in certain jeopardy, I would think God would forgive abortion in those circumstances. I think if a young woman, scared, confused, made the decision to abort, God would be understanding and forgiving. Most intelligent mature women have options; birth control, abstinence, those are their rights and responsibilities. The Lord wants us, I believe, to be responsible for ourselves, our lives, our bodies. We must be accountable for our actions and our sins. I am not trying to judge anyone who has had an abortion. God loves you and if you make a mistake and find this is your only way out I am sure God will be understanding and merciful. But, if you have a cavalier attitude that, "So what I will just do what I want! It is my body and I will just get another abortion." I don't think God will smile on you again! I'm not saying you will be sentenced to eternal damnation, but God wants us to respect his laws and us. What kind of respect are you paying to yourself, or God, by throwing away a precious potential human being, like it was so much unwanted garbage!

There is so much at risk with our sexual freedoms. We have AIDs, incurable venereal disease, herpes and a woman afflicted with chlymidia could be rendered, never able to bear children! There is prostitution, legal in some countries, in our state of Nevada! Believe me dear reader, what goes on in Vegas, does not stay in Vegas! God sees our ever increasing moral degradation, which is not acceptable to God. Women and men are selling more than their bodies. They are selling bit by bit their self-esteem and their very souls!

So, I implore all those struggling to reach out for help. If you feel lost, there are churches everywhere where you can pray and be heard. If you truly want to find the right answers or path, God, Jesus, and his Angels, will gladly guide you away from darkness and evil. Remember, dear reader, if you continually steer in a positive direction, making positive healthy choices and trying to find the good in others, you will lead an enriched life, one where you will feel good about you and others. Sexual promiscuity, having abortions without any thought or care about the unborn is a negative path and one not acceptable to God.

CHAPTER FOURTEEN:
SCIENTOLOGY AN ALIEN RELIGION

In Exodus; verse 20: God said: "You must not have any other gods except me." You must not worship or serve any idol, because I, the Lord your God, am a jealous God. If you hate me, then I will punish your children, and even your grandchildren and great grandchildren. But I show kindness to thousands who love me and obey my commands."

So, I do not think God is smiling on Scientologists! They have established churches and consider their beliefs a religion. I ask you who do they worship? Not God certainly! I would say any so called religion that excludes the Lord Almighty and his only son, Lord Jesus is not a religion but a dangerous cult! Dear reader, this 'so called religion' was created by a science fiction writer, L. Ron Hubbard. Hubbard created this religion in December 1953. Hubbard served in the U.S. Navy during W.W.II and appeared to fancy himself as a military hero, though he served with no marked distinction. He would have his most zealous followers, dress in seafaring uniforms and they were called the 'Sea Org'. They would show their faith by signing billion year contracts. These contracts demonstrated their devotions to serve for the next billion years in future reincarnations. These scientologists believed they were immortal gods or "thetans" who lived for millions of years and would continued to be reincarnated for millions of years to come.

Scientologist believe that a human is an immortal alien, spiritual being or "thetan" that is trapped on earth in a physical body. The thetan is believed to have had numerous past lives and that life before the thetan arrived on the earth, was lived in 'extra-terrestrial' cultures. They believe that a series of events occurred before life on earth and that humans have hidden abilities that can be unlocked and the person can achieve greater spiritual awareness.

To achieve greater spiritual awareness, they embrace a tool known as 'auditing' which is a tool to find out all of a member's weaknesses and I ask you what better way to control them? They have the audacity to use the Christian cross with a star-like symbol behind it to try and legitimize their farce as a religion! A religion based on greed and control is no religion. Many journalists, courts and governing bodies of several countries have stated that the Church of Scientology is a cult and an unscrupulous commercial enterprise that harasses its critics and misuses the trust of its members. You probably heard the ranting of Tom Cruise in his interview with Matt Lauer. Scientologists are adamantly opposed to Psychiatry. Tom Cruise appears to be a decent human being and caring husband and father but he is being grossly misled by this 'so called religion'. I have been a mental health professional for over 25 years and while I don't agree with everything Psychiatry has to offer, it has done far more good than harm. A person suffering from Bipolar Disorder or Schizophrenia needs more than special vitamins to be well let me tell you. It is so obvious to me that Mr. Cruise, though certainly entitled to his opinion, needs to stick to his acting because he clearly lacks the knowledge or expertise to be judging Psychiatry. I don't know how he could abandon his love of God for Scientology but he and others like him are playing a dangerous game. It appears Satan, the father of all lies, will have the last laugh on them. Make no mistake, as I have stressed in this book, you have but one life to live, (there is no reincarnation), one's soul, given by God himself, and if you live a life apart from God, you diminish that soul or the very essence of you. Some of you will diminish your soul to the point it will be extinguished forever! God created the Universe, and is all-powerful, he creates matter and he alone can destroy it!

I, like God would like to save souls. I am not in anyway trying to say I am on the same footing as the Almighty, but I love people and hate to see anyone throw away their immortal soul. Certainly there are controversial religions out there and I caution if you are not worshiping the Lord God Almighty and Jesus, his only Son, who sacrificed his life, suffered on the cross and died so you could have everlasting life, then you are in grave spiritual danger, make no mistake! As, God has stated, he is a jealous God, and any that would chose another god or worship anyone or anything else will not be in his favor, will not enter his Kingdom!

CHAPTER FIFTEEN:
THREE KEYS TO HAPPINESS

Dear reader, stop buying all of those self-help books! This is all you need to know about finding true happiness! The three keys to happiness are: 1. Love and believe in God and Jesus. 2. Love and believe in yourself. 3. Have a sense of humor. If you truly follow these, all good will follow. To love and believe in God and Jesus means just that. You fully trust in and believe in the Almighty and Lord Jesus and pray to them when hurt, in trouble or just to feel closer. You accept God as the Supreme Being, the ruler of the universe and respect his laws and teachings of him and his only son, Lord Jesus. A person, who loves God, loves himself, respects himself and therefore, can more easily love and respect others, regardless of how much money they have or the color of their skin! A person, who loves God and Jesus, knows they want what is best for them. God has angels far superior to man, who guides the righteous, leaders, scientists to develop technology, medical advances to help man live longer and better. There are some radical so called religious groups who shun medical science and may refuse life saving blood transfusions to die instead, because they feel it is not in keeping with their so-called religion. God would never expect a person who has access to expert medical care to refuse this for their child or loved one and choose certain death! God is merciful and wants us to use our wisdom to help and nurture ourselves and others and not harm them! When we love ourselves we choose any positive means to better ourselves, through the advances in medicine, psychology, psychiatry or technology. We should all feel free to pray or seek out any positive means to help ourselves. When we love ourselves we want to be around others who love God and themselves and have decent morals. So, you would shun toxic relationships and not allow others to control or abuse you.

Finally, yes, a sense of humor. Yes, life is serious business, we have important decisions and tasks to do daily, but we must not take ourselves too seriously. The Lord wants us to be happy and be able to laugh at ourselves at times and find humor when we can. As they say, laughter really can be the best medicine! So, love God, Jesus, yourself and others, and laugh with them and you will likely live longer, lead a more fulfilled life in this one and the next to come!

CHAPTER SIXTEEN:
MESSAGE TO THE CATHOLIC CHURCH

There was a time not long ago, when almost every time you picked up a newspaper there were articles about Catholic priests who had allegedly sexually abused a child or young adult. These were ordained priests who read and studied God's laws and sacred readings in the Bible. They listened to other's confessions! And who would listen to theirs?

In a recent New York Times article, it reports that an Irish bishop resigned after an abuse report. The Vatican accepted the resignation of the bishop of Limerick, Donal Brendan Murray, and 69 years old. The Irish government report criticized the Catholic hierarchy for failing to act and covering up complaints of 320 children who were alleged to have been sexually abused by priests between 1974 and 2004.

Pope Benedict XVI urged Irish bishops to show determination and resolve in confronting the sexual abuse scandal, but made no call for the punishment of the perpetrators.

A message I received from heaven and I believe from Jesus, himself, was: "To suppress or abstain from the normal is to invite the abnormal." In other words priests ordained do not marry and therefore, must abstain from the very normal healthy desires all humans are given. Why? You may wonder, does God the Almighty expect this of those who spread the Good News. The answer, dear reader is "No", he does not. In the Bible, Leviticus (21:7), New Century Version; it says a priest must not marry an unclean prostitute or a divorced woman, because he is holy to his God. Also in Leviticus versus (13-14), New Century Version" The high priest must marry a woman who is a virgin. He must not marry a widow, a divorced woman, or a prostitute. I am the Lord; I have set the high priest apart for his special job."

I do not see why the Catholic Church deems this necessary for a man who wants to serve God. A marriage between a man and a woman is a holy union blessed by God. I believe a man can devote to his church and his bride and be all the better for both, because he has his spiritual needs ever uplifted by this very devoted service to God and he is more enriched by joining in deep love and devotion to his bride. In Luke (16:13), New Century Version, it says; "You cannot serve both God and worldly riches." God does not say you cannot serve me if you are married.

Dear reader, I have every respect for the Pope, and the leaders of the Catholic Church, or any church that preaches the Good News and promotes the Almighty and his only son, Lord Jesus. But, dear reader, I do know these abuses have not just happened recently, they have been going on for centuries! We only are now becoming more aware of this because of our expansive media outlets and modern technological advances of the internet, radio, television satellites. So, I just wish the leaders of the Catholic Church, most notably the Pope, himself, would take this into consideration, because, though they plan to screen more carefully, this will still continue to be a problem. No matter what the religion, there will be leaders, priests, ministers, those in great authority who will use their power over others to commit sin and God knows all, sees all, and they will indeed be punished eventually. They will be punished, if not in this life, definitely in the next. But, I ask if allowing priests to marry could curtail this most hateful sin, why not allow it?

CHAPTER SEVENTEEN:
HONOR KILLINGS LEAVE NO HONOR

Many radical Muslims believe it is sanctioned by God to kill their own flesh and blood, this is known as honor killing. If a family member does something that they feel brings shame, dishonor, and humiliation to the family, then they feel they are justified in killing that family member. A young woman may fall in love with a man not of the family's religion, may start to dress and act in ways "too Western," or may actually have sex before marriage; these acts could result in their death.

According to the U.N., honor killing has been reported in Egypt, Jordan, Lebanon, Morocco, Pakistan, the Syrian Arab Republic, Turkey, Yemen and other Persian Gulf countries. It is also found in western countries within migrant communities in France, Germany, and the United Kingdom.

It is difficult to obtain precise statistics as many crimes are never reported and frequently those murdered in honor killings are recorded as having committed suicide or having died in accidents.

In 2008, a Saudi woman was killed by her father for chatting on Facebook to a man. In Istanbul, a 2008 report by the Turkish Prime Ministry Human Rights Directorate, indicated there is one honor killing every week over 1,000 in the last five years. UNICEF reports in Gaza strip and the West Bank more that two third of all murders were likely honor killings. Every year in the UK, a dozen women are victims of honor killing. In Pakistan, honor killing is called Karo-Kari.

In 2003, in Pakistan, 1,261 women were murdered in honor killings. In November 2006, a bill was passed to strengthen the law against honor killing, but Women's Rights groups are doubtful the law will actually help women.

God forgives us for our sins and wants us to be forgiving of others. In Luke (17:4), "If he sins against you seven times in one day and says that he is sorry each time, forgive him." The Lord Almighty would not sanction these killings. Lord Jesus has said, "Let he who is without sin, cast the first stone!" They do not bring any honor to the family only disgrace. By killing their very own child, someone they should be loving, understanding and protecting, they break God's law. The child departed from his/her earthly existence will go to Heaven and be surrounded by the glowing loving light of God. But beware to those who violate God's teachings of love and forgiveness, those who ruthlessly, unmercifully murder their own child will face the wrath of God like no other!

I want to ask them is it really worth your very soul and life everlasting in Heaven? Remember the Devil hates women and when woman are victimized like this, the devil laughs in delight. Many are stoned to death for things they have never done! God is watching and that is why the path is wide that leads to Hell!

CHAPTER EIGHTEEN:
THE FATHER OF LIES AND DEATH
VS THE FATHER OF TRUTH AND
EVERLASTING LIFE

So dear reader, I mean no disrespect to you or your religion but I am telling you the truth. It comes from Heaven to me to you. I am not suffering from delusions of grandeur or psychoses. I am psychic, not psychotic! I believe I have been chosen by God and Jesus to convey these messages to you. When I started wearing my cross necklace a few years back, God was pleased. One evening as I was about to fall asleep, I saw a vision so clear! It was a beautiful pair of large hands. The hands appeared masculine and dangling from the one hand was a glittering silver cross necklace. The cross was somewhat large, maybe about two inches long, very shiny silver. There was a bright glowing light about the hands and necklace. God was pleased. Jesus died on the cross for our sins, he rose from the dead and ascended into Heaven, to be seated at the right hand of God Almighty. He did not; as psychic, Sylvia Browne, might have you believe, survive, marry and have children. Sylvia Browne, in her book, "The Mystical Life of Jesus", would have you believe this nonsense and that the Devil does not exist, that God is always loving and never angry or punishing. She would have you believe there is reincarnation. Dear reader, these are dangerous beliefs, and much of what she espouses comes from her spirit guide "Francine", a.k.a. the Devil! He is the father of all lies and he has found the perfect fool! I am sorry Sylvia, but this is everything the Devil wants us to believe! Sin, you'll get another lifetime to make it right. God is a loving God, and will not punish you. She would have you believe that the Devil, Hell, they do not exist and you should not fear you will end up there no matter what sins you commit! She says Jesus was a nice man who was spreading good teachings but was not the Son of God! Yes, reader, believe all of these lies and you are buying yourself a one way ticket to Hell!

Yes, dear reader, the Lord loves, is slow to anger, but if you read the Bible, you will see countless references to God's anger toward those who follow the sinful path. Sodom and Gomorrah were two cities filled with sin and God had had enough and all the sinners were destroyed with the cities! So, I tell you there is but one God and his only son, Jesus Christ. The Lord has his Angels and lives in a beautiful Kingdom called Heaven. Then you have Satan and his demons. I have seen some of the demons as I had indicated earlier, walking with inverted crosses. They are in Hell and in this world. The Angels attempt to guide the righteous, to do God's work, but the Devil and his demons guide man to go against God's commandments, to lie, sin, steal, murder, commit adultery, lust for power and money and do anything to get it.

Dear reader, just look at our world today, giant corporations, banks and businesses folding across our nation and the globe! There is war, terror, murder and mayhem. I ask you if these men, women that help cause this strife and sin had followed God's laws, would the world be in this sad state? Of course not! When I finished this chapter, I got a message from Heaven, he said, and I believe it was Jesus, "smart". If you, as a person, turn from God, do not accept the truth, that Jesus is God's son then you may be doomed. If us, as a nation, turns from God, we are doomed!

CHAPTER NINETEEN:
A SOUL IS A TERRIBLE THING TO WASTE

Dear reader, if you remember anything from reading this book, remember this, that this is the testing ground to determine your fitness for everlasting life! You have only one soul, one life here on earth. If you live the normal life span, it is not that long. As they say, life is short and yours may be shorter than you think. You may have been living an empty sinful all for me, hell with tomorrow lifestyle. You may have no remorse or repentance and tomorrow you may become gravely ill or be killed in an accident. Where will you go from there? Well if you do not believe in God and accept Jesus as his son, our Savior, then you may be looking at eternal damnation with Satan. Remember, as I have stated, the road is long and the gates wide that leads to Hell. When we look at the evil leaders of some of the nations, the evil Ahmadinejad of Iran, Il Jong, of North Korea, the evil hate-mongers; Neo-Nazis, skinheads, those who traffic drugs and humans, spread terror, we can see why this is so stated in the Bible. I am sure if Jesus were walking about in the world today, he would not be dropping by one of Osama bin Laden's terrorist training camps and be patting him on the back, saying: "Oh excellent, Osama, and how many innocents have you blown up today?"!

Remember it all boils down to Good vs. Evil, God vs. Satan. When you read the world news today it is easy to see who stands with God and who stands with the Devil. The Devil wants to destroy man, his life and all that is good and breed anger, hatred, resentments, jealousy and greed. He hates women and you read about the extensive mass murdering in parts of Africa, the thousands of women raped and murdered. Satan's playmates to be sure and what will be their reward in the end? The dark pit of Hell and Satan laughing gleefully and repeating in their ears for all eternity, "I've got you now!" Remember that there will be no options ever, we are talking about eternal, forever damnation! But, for those who loved God and accept Jesus, there is paradise. You are young again, no cares or worries, in a beautiful place of indescribable beauty and positive energy and peace.

People, this is simple, it is not rocket science, and you are either aligned with God or aligned with the Devil. You are human, God recognizes you will slip up from time to time and sin, but if you, with all your heart and soul are truly sorry and repent, he is and can be most forgiving and merciful. He knows what is truly in your heart and mind, but so does Satan. If you are filled with hatred, then Satan will guide you to the pit or maybe the destruction of your very soul! You have free will. You may have had a tough life, parents not there for you, poverty and many setbacks, but there is always God and Jesus. They are there to guide you on the path to a brighter life. It is your choice and I hope you will choose the love of God and Jesus. A soul is a terrible thing to waste. It is your gift from God. You can choose to nourish and enrich it with love and forgiveness or blacken and wither it, with hatred and greed!

ABOUT THE AUTHOR

Ms Miller is a medium who has extraordinary psychic abilities and has had thousands of psychic/paranormal experiences with the spiritual realm since the age of twelve. Her experiences are very unique and profound. She will provide answers to many of mankind's most probing questions in regard to heaven, hell and life after death. She lives in the St. Louis area.